HOW TO DEAL

HOW TO DEAL

with Fear, Failure, and Other Daily Dreads

Grace Miceli

VORACIOUS
Little, Brown and Company
New York Boston London

Voracious / Little, Brown and Company
Hachette Book Group
1290 Avenue of the Americas, New York, NY 10104
littlebrown.com

First Edition: May 2021

Voracious is an imprint of Little, Brown and Company, a division of Hachette Book Group, Inc. The Voracious name and logo are trademarks of Hachette Book Group, Inc.

The publisher is not responsible for websites (or their content) that are not owned by the publisher.

The Hachette Speakers Bureau provides a wide range of authors for speaking events. To find out more, go to hachettespeakersbureau.com or call (866) 376-6591.

Photography/artwork by Grace Miceli

ISBN 978-0-316-59248-2
LCCN 2020952600

Printing 1, 2021

LSC-C

Printed in the United States of America

♥ FOR TONY

Contents

Introduction

I'd like to start with a disclaimer: I am not a mental health professional. Despite its prescriptive title (also a reference to a film starring my favorite pop star of the early aughts), this book is full of questions. How do we come to terms with everything that we have to face? How the heck do we deal?

I've been fumbling around trying to manage my mental health for a while, and I'm starting to find my way thanks to outside help, access to resources, and a frustratingly overwhelming amount of self-examination. I'd like to share what I've found along the way. My hope is that maybe one page can provide you with temporary relief or a moment of connection; I want you to feel seen.

There is no one way to deal, no quick fix. We can shift our perspectives, feel our feelings, and communicate assertively, but there are still oppressive systems and structures of power to contend with. We all must learn to deal with our individual traumas while facing our external circumstances and managing our interactions with others. It's a mess around here.

The majority of these illustrations were created during lockdown when we weren't able to hug our friends or have a passive-aggressive meal with our parents. Some days, I'd worry I'd forgotten how to have a conversation with another human being. I'd try my best to find the light where I could. As in, letting myself off the hook for not being able to text someone back for a week while simultaneously checking who liked my dog's Instagram post multiple times every hour. I'm a complicated person and so are you.

I'm not here asking you to fix yourself. There's nothing wrong with you, okay? I know that how my day goes depends on whether I wake up full of hope or despair. It's not about what's happening, it's about my relationship to what's happening, you know? And right now, I have to feel hopeful that by sharing what follows—by showing up as a vulnerable, fallible, and very-much-still-working-on-it person—it will be less scary for me to keep trying to be present, and maybe it can inspire you to do the same. I have to be hopeful that each day can be different and better. I'm grateful to be able to create something from all of the fear and anxiety and pain and joy and say "Hey! I'm here! This is me, this is what I see and know and what I want to learn and maybe we can help each other do that." One thing I do know is that we need each other to get through it and to deal.

Chapter 1
How to Not Make It Personal

You know what's really weird? Not everything is about you. I know, I know, I didn't believe it at first either. The most terrifying yet freeing fact that I learned in my late twenties (it's still sinking in) is that you have the choice to not take everything personally, including but not limited to: the eye roll a stranger gives you when you walk by them on the street; the comment an acquaintance makes about how you look tired and/or sick; or your great-aunt's questions about why you're still single. We are constantly screaming our insecurities out loud at each other by way of well-meaning advice, judgmental stares, or "innocent enough" questions. Projecting isn't cute but we love to do it, and these comments can cut deep.

But what if you stopped giving so much weight to other people's opinions?

Sometimes I realize I don't even stop to think about what *I* think before just assuming everyone else's views are definite and true and more grounded in reality than mine. I'm not saying this to absolve you of being mindful of what you say and do (please continue doing that). But I think life would be a little easier if we could stop assuming that what everyone else does is a reflection on us.

You can't control other people's reactions or perceptions, no matter how hard you try. I've tried. I've failed. And after years of therapy, reading all the self-help books, taking countless workshops, listening to one million podcasts, and spending way too much time in my head reflecting, I'm finally learning that the only thing I can control is my response to other people. The way I choose to react when someone I have a crush on doesn't text me back or when that dream freelance client doesn't end up offering me the job, or when my friends hang out and don't invite me—that's what I can control. I can take the time to pause, realize this isn't about me, and then not immediately dive headfirst into a spiral of insecurity and panic. I highly recommend diving into fewer insecurity and panic spirals. Life's more fun that way.

ISN'T IT ANNOYING

WHEN OTHER PEOPLE

DON'T DO WHAT

YOU WANT THEM TO?

TO-DO LIST

- FIND HEADPHONES

- BUY LAUNDRY DETERGENT

- STOP TAKING RESPONSIBILITY FOR OTHER PEOPLE'S FEELINGS

- SHAVE LEGS

DEAR DIARY,
DO YOU EVER
THINK ABOUT
HOW THE THINGS
THAT BOTHER YOU
ABOUT OTHER
PEOPLE ARE OFTEN
THE THINGS YOU
FEAR MAY BE
TRUE ABOUT
YOURSELF? MAYBE
IT'S JUST ME.

13

MY TOP 5 FAVORITE QUESTIONS TO ASK MYSELF IN THE MIDDLE OF THE NIGHT WHEN I CAN'T SLEEP

ARE YOU MAD AT ME?

EXACTLY WHEN, HOW, AND WHERE WILL I DIE?

WHY AM I ME AND NOT YOU?

ARE VAMPIRES REAL?

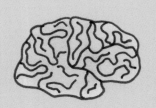

WHAT ARE THE LIMITS OF MY DOG'S CONSCIOUSNESS?

TO-DO LIST

- CHIROPRACTOR @ 11 A.M.

- LAUNDRY

- CONVINCE EVERY PERSON I HAVE EVER MET AND WILL EVER MEET TO LIKE ME

BE CAREFUL NOT

TO LET

THEIR   JUDGMENT

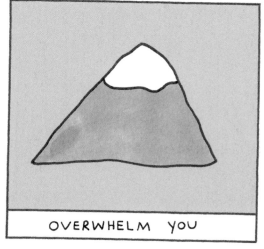

OVERWHELM YOU

DEAR DIARY,
I JUST HEARD
THAT YOU DON'T
HAVE TO RELY
ON EXTERNAL
VALIDATION FOR
YOUR SELF-ESTEEM.
IF THIS IS
TRUE, IT LIKE
TOTALLY CHANGES
EVERYTHING.

LITTLE PIECES OF
DOG TREATS

HAND SANITIZER

THE LETTER I WROTE
MY PARENTS IN 1997
TRYING TO CONVINCE
THEM TO LET ME WATCH
"TITANIC" (IT DID NOT
WORK)

A SINGLE
POTATO CHIP

HOT PINK LIPSTICK I
HAVE HAD FOR 3 YEARS
AND NEVER WORN BUT
I AM HOPEFUL STILL

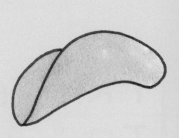

WHAT'S IN MY BAG?

A Guide to People-Pleasing Total Strangers

(IN CASE IT DOES NOT COME NATURALLY TO YOU)

ON PHONE CALLS, ALWAYS SPEAK IN THE HIGHEST POSSIBLE VOICE SO THEY KNOW YOU'RE LIKE SUPER NICE

IF YOU'RE SITTING NEXT TO SOMEONE ON THE TRAIN AND SUDDENLY LOTS OF SPACE OPENS UP - DON'T MOVE! WHOEVER IS SITTING NEXT TO YOU MIGHT TAKE IT PERSONALLY

A. A. W. E.

(ALWAYS AGREE WITH EVERYONE)

SCREAM "I'M SORRY" DURING AND/OR AFTER ALL SLIGHTLY UNCOMFORTABLE INTERACTIONS

WHEN A SALES ASSOCIATE TELLS YOU IT LOOKS GOOD, YOU HAVE TO BUY IT, THAT'S THE RULE

WHEN SOMEONE GIVES YOU A COMPLIMENT DEFLECT IMMEDIATELY AND REPLY WITH A WAY BIGGER COMPLIMENT

RUN AWAY QUICKLY WHEN SOMETHING WEIRD HAPPENS SO THAT NO ONE REMEMBERS YOUR FACE

YOU CAN'T CONTROL

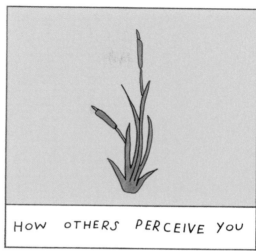

HOW OTHERS PERCEIVE YOU

SO YOU MIGHT AS WELL DO

WHATEVER YOU WANT BECAUSE THIS IS KINDA IT, YOU KNOW?

I WONDER WHAT
IT'S LIKE FOR THEM
OVER THERE?

PROBABLY GOOD AND
BAD AND OFTEN BOTH
AT THE SAME TIME.

25

I'VE REALIZED I'M MOST AFRAID OF

THE THOUGHTS I
HAVE ABOUT MYSELF

DEAR DIARY,

IT'S OK THAT THERE ARE PEOPLE WHO CAN DO STUFF BETTER THAN I CAN.

WHAT I WOULD DO IF I WASN'T SO BUSY THINKING ABOUT WHAT YOU MIGHT BE THINKING ABOUT

START A CHIHUAHUA RESCUE FARM UPSTATE

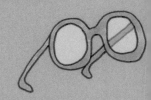

LEARN ENOUGH ABOUT PLANTS TO KEEP MOST (SOME?) OF THEM ALIVE

EXPAND MY COLLECTION OF GRANDMA GLASSES

WRITE A YOUNG ADULT FANTASY NOVEL ABOUT THE DAUGHTER OF A MOB BOSS WHO FALLS IN LOVE WITH A VAMPIRE, THINK "TWILIGHT" MEETS "THE SOPRANOS"

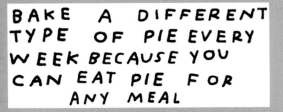

BAKE A DIFFERENT TYPE OF PIE EVERY WEEK BECAUSE YOU CAN EAT PIE FOR ANY MEAL

TO-DO LIST

- SHOWER

- DROP OFF PACKAGES AT POST OFFICE

- GIVE EVERYONE IN MY LIFE ADVICE THAT I SHOULD BE TELLING MYSELF INSTEAD

- ORGANIZE JUNK DRAWER

Practical Advice

FOR WHEN YOU'RE STUCK IN A NEGATIVE AND/OR PAINFUL THOUGHT PATTERN

SPLASH YOUR FACE WITH COLD WATER

1. MY THERAPIST
2. TAKING BREAKS FROM THE INTERNET
3. MY FRIENDS
4. ICE CREAM
5. MAKING LISTS

WRITE A LIST OF THINGS YOU ARE GRATEFUL FOR

4EVER

CHECK THE TRACKING NUMBERS OF EVERYTHING YOU BOUGHT ONLINE LAST WEEK

WATCH AN ENTIRE SEASON
OF YOUR FAVORITE SHOW
FROM WHEN YOU WERE
16 AND ONLY HAD 2 FRIENDS

HANG OUT WITH SOME
TREES OR FLOWERS

OPEN UP YOUR WINDOW
AND SCREAM

MAKE S'MORES

THERE HAVE BEEN TIMES WHEN I'VE REALIZED THAT I'VE CHASED THINGS

IN AN ATTEMPT TO IMPRESS OR PLEASE OTHERS, ONLY TO DISCOVER THAT

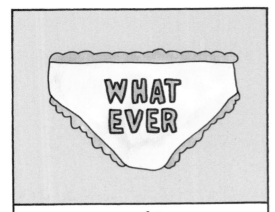

WHAT EVER

THEY DIDN'T REALLY CARE - NOT THAT THEY DIDN'T CARE ABOUT ME BUT THAT

I WAS ACTING OUT OF FEAR OF AN IMAGINED POTENTIAL JUDGMENT

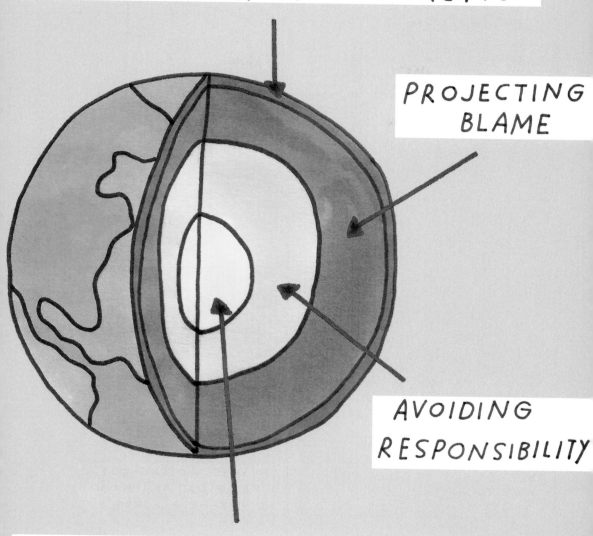

WHEN I'M SCARED OR OVERWHELMED

I DON'T NEED ADVICE OR FOR YOU TO TRY AND FIX THINGS

WHAT FEELS THE BEST IS

WHEN YOU JUST SIT WITH ME AND LISTEN

GROCERY LIST

- BROCCOLI

- RECOGNITION THAT JUST BECAUSE I HAVE A THOUGHT IT DOESN'T MEAN IT'S TRUE

- HOT SAUCE (GREEN ONE)

WHEN I FIND MYSELF

SPEAKING NEGATIVELY
ABOUT SOMEONE

I HAVE TO LISTEN
CLOSELY BECAUSE

I'M MOST LIKELY
TALKING ABOUT MYSELF

DEAR DIARY,

CAN I REALLY TRUST MYSELF? I KNOW THAT I'M SUPPOSED TO LISTEN TO MY INTUITION BUT WHAT IF IT'S SCARED OF EVERYTHING?

Things to Do Instead of Projecting Your Insecurities onto Other People

WALK YOUR DOG

RELEASE THE SCARY THOUGHTS IN YOUR HEAD BY JOURNALING FOR 3-5 PAGES DEPENDING ON THE DAY

BRUSH YOUR TEETH

WRITE TO YOUR
GRANDMA

CALL YOUR BEST FRIEND

EAT SPAGHETTI AND
MEATBALLS

GO OUTSIDE AND STARE INTO
THE SKY AND REMEMBER THAT
YOU ARE A SMALL PART OF A
VERY BIG THING IN A TOTALLY
COOL AND COMFORTING WAY

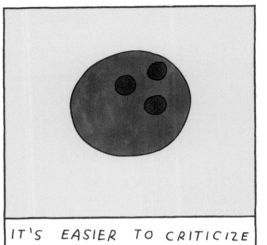

IT'S EASIER TO CRITICIZE

THINGS ABOUT YOU

THAT I SEE AND

DON'T LIKE IN ME

Chapter 2
How to Stay When You Want to Run Away

Something I find myself doing every 15 minutes or so is picking up my phone and cycling through the same few apps multiple times in a row. I know there is an extremely low probability of a life-changing email or Instagram follow needing immediate attention, but still I find myself chasing these momentary dopamine rushes way more than I would like to admit. If I take a break from the internet, will everyone forget that I exist? When I'm busy everything seems fine, but when there is an afternoon with nothing to do the dread begins to creep in.

Being fully present with yourself or work or friends or family or partner or chihuahua can be kind of terrifying. I love to look for ways to escape so that I don't have to face reality; my favorite way of doing this is by diving headlong into an analysis of any of the confusing or overwhelming or conflicting feelings that I might be having. I have come to realize that instead of checking in with myself (because that would mean taking responsibility for my thoughts and actions), this was a way of hiding underneath a blanket made from a 50 percent avoidance and 50 percent fear-of-everything fabric blend.

This avoidance might also manifest as: googling my ex-best friend from middle school; eating two boxes of girl scout cookies in a single day; color-coding my books; drinking lots of alcohol all the time; online shopping late at night for a third color of the exact same jumpsuit I have already have; waking and baking and then going to the gym to walk slowly on the treadmill while watching Bravo; asking someone a question and then not listening to their answer; looking up the relationship history of the entire cast of whatever I'm watching while I'm watching it; scrolling through photos of my dog while I'm sitting next to him; hanging out with my friends every free moment I have; and the constant phone checking thing I mentioned before. None of these coping mechanisms are inherently bad (who am I to judge?), but they also aren't all that helpful when you're trying to figure out who you are and what kind of life you want to lead. All of your feelings are valid, but let's be real: there are healthy and unhealthy ways of expressing them.

Are you really here right now, or are you just kind of skimming all these sentences? How does the paper feel between your fingers when you turn the page? Have you picked out a favorite drawing yet? Maybe it's too early to decide, that's okay, no pressure. Are you thinking about what you're going to order for dinner tonight or that email you forgot to send this morning? That's okay, me too.

FIRST I CLOSE THE

APP AND THEN

I OPEN IT

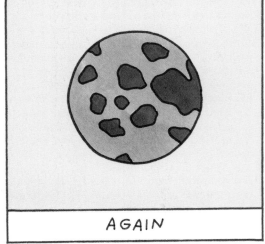

AGAIN

44

I CAN HAVE A HARD TIME STAYING IN MY BODY. HOW CAN I KNOW WHAT I REALLY FEEL WHEN I ONLY HANG OUT IN MY HEAD?

HISTORY

RECENTLY CLOSED

- 🌐 EXERCISE WITHOUT SWEATING
- 📷 INSTAGRAM
- 🌐 HOW TO STOP INTERRUPTING PEOPLE
- 🏦 TD BANK
- 🌐 CAN MY DOWNSTAIRS NEIGHBOR HEAR ME FART?

RECENTLY VISITED

- ▶️ ANIMALS REUNITING WITH THEIR OWNERS
- 📷 INSTAGRAM
- 🌐 WHY CAN'T I CRY?
- ▶️ KEANU REEVES' MOST ROMANTIC SCENES
- 📷 INSTAGRAM
- 🌐 WHAT IF MY DOG IS LITERALLY MY BEST FRIEND?
- 📷 INSTAGRAM

IS THERE ANYTHING

THAT YOU

CAN AVOID

FOREVER?

DEAR DIARY,
I'VE HAD A LOT
ON MY MIND LATELY.
I'VE BEEN THINKING
ABOUT HOW IF I'M
SCARED TO TALK
ABOUT SOMETHING,
THAT PROBABLY
MEANS I REALLY NEED
TO. I WANT TO
PAY ATTENTION TO
WHAT MAKES ME

UNCOMFORTABLE,
AND THAT IT'S
IMPORTANT TO
REMEMBER: I
OFTEN FEEL
CLOSER WHENEVER
I HAVE A DIFFICULT
CONVERSATION WITH
SOMEONE. BUT
SOMETIMES AFTER
I FEEL FARTHER
AWAY.

Feeling
LONELY IS
Totally Normal
80 Liquid Filled Capsules
STOP AVOIDING IT

I Just Feel Like

I'M HOLDING ON TO A RAPIDLY ASCENDING HOT AIR BALLOON BUT IN A TOTALLY SAFE WAY WHEN I'M EXCITED

MY BODY IS A WARM CINNAMON BUN WITH LOTS OF ICING WHEN I'M COMPASSIONATE

I'M A VERY PRICKLY CACTUS THAT HAS SET ITSELF ON FIRE WHEN I'M ANGRY

I'M WEARING ONE OF THOSE
SLEEPING BAG COATS BUT
IT'S MADE OF CLOUDS
WHEN I'M CALM

I'M BEING CHASED BY A
PACK OF HUNGRY WOLVES
AND I CAN'T RUN THAT
FAST WHEN I'M AFRAID

I'M LYING IN A FIELD
OF FLOWERS THAT IS
ABOUT TO BLOOM
WHEN I'M HOPEFUL

THERE IS A GIANT
CRASHING WAVE
IN MY STOMACH
WHEN I'M SAD

I THOUGHT THAT IF I FILLED MY
HOME WITH THINGS IT WOULD
NOT FEEL EMPTY ANYMORE

I'M ALWAYS JUMPING

AHEAD OR LOOKING

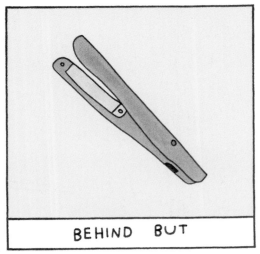

BEHIND BUT

WHAT'S RIGHT HERE ?

Worry About It Tomorrow!

I'M OFTEN CONVINCED
THAT HAVING NEW
THINGS WILL MAKE ME A

NEW PERSON AND IT'S SO
FUN TO HAVE SOMETHING
TO LOOK FORWARD TO

BUT WHEN IT ARRIVES
I REALIZE THAT I'M
EXACTLY THE SAME

I JUST HAVE
MORE STUFF NOW

59

DEAR DIARY,

TODAY I'M SAD BUT TOMORROW I MIGHT NOT BE.

OK, WELL, THAT'S ALL FOR NOW.

Your Comfort Zone May Be a Trap

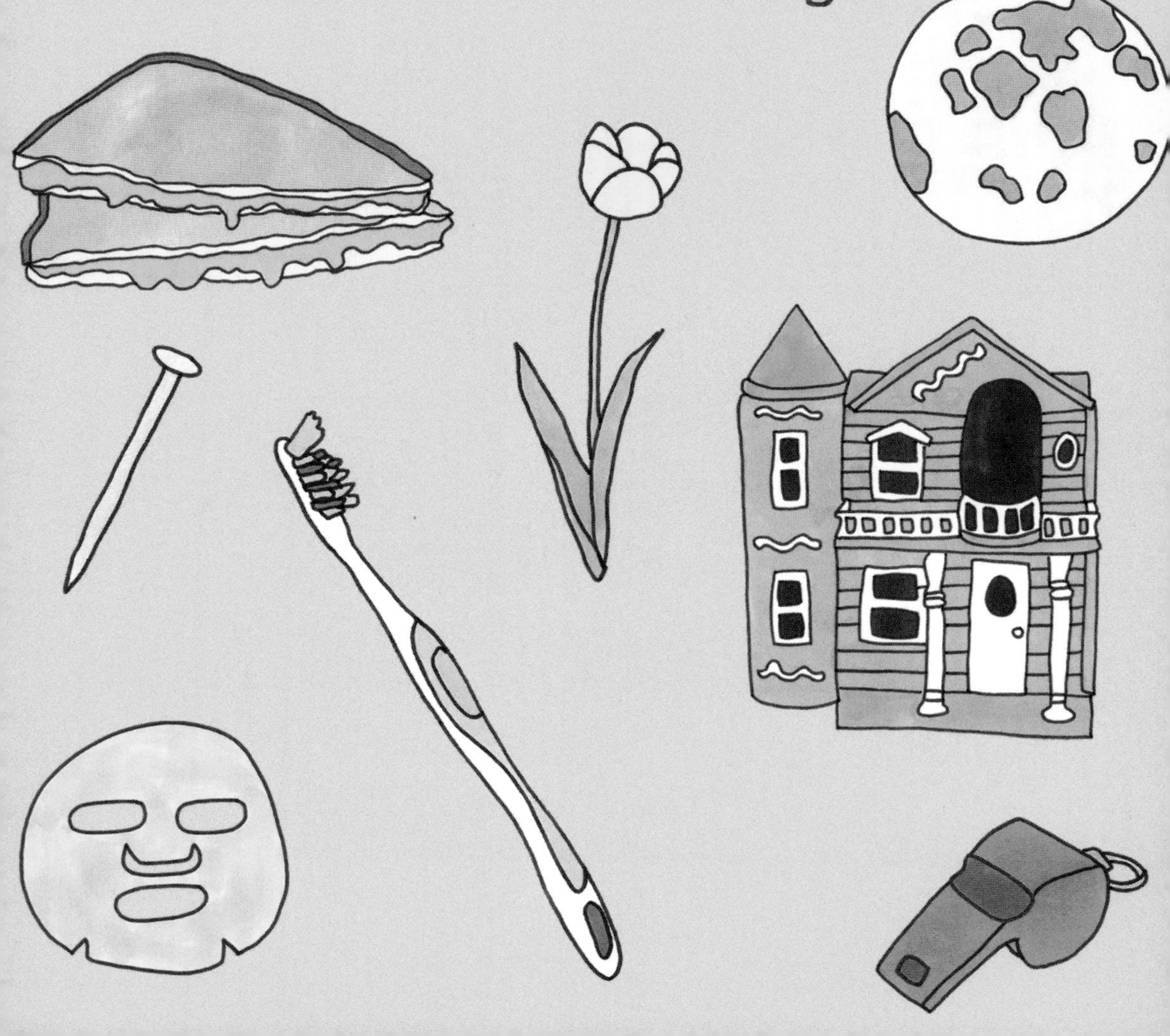

I WISH I COULD PUT INTO WORDS

WHAT I'M FEELING

WHEN I JUMP TOO QUICKLY

I PANIC

I FORGET THAT

I COULD BE CURIOUS INSTEAD

IF YOU NEED TO YOU CAN
TAKE THE TIME TO FIND

A PLACE TO HIDE

SOME DAYS I DON'T REALLY WANT TO BE MYSELF AND WOULD RATHER BE

MY PILLOW: SO THAT I NEVER HAVE TO SLEEP ALONE

THE ICE CREAM IN MY FREEZER: DESIRED AND NECESSARY FOR A JOYFUL EXISTENCE

THE PLANT ON MY DESK: I'D GET TO HEAR ALL OF THE EXCITING IDEAS BUT NOT HAVE TO DO ANY OF THE WORK

MY PHONE : ENDLESS ATTENTION

A STAMP: A LIFE FULL OF TRAVEL AND PURPOSE WITHOUT TAKING UP TOO MUCH SPACE

USA FOREVER

I LIKE IT WHEN

MY PHONE SAYS

"YOU'RE ALL CAUGHT UP"

AND I KEEP GOING

71

THINGS TO DO THAT ARE MOST LIKELY MORE FUN THAN WHAT YOU SHOULD BE DOING RIGHT NOW

Let's Get Distracted!

SHAPE YOUR EYEBROWS, TRY SOMETHING NEW! THE TINY SHORT ONES YOU HAD IN MIDDLE SCHOOL WERE AWESOME

NEATLY REFOLD ALL THE CLOTHES IN YOUR DRESSER AS IF YOU WON'T SHOVE THEM BACK IN AFTER TRYING ON FIVE OUTFITS TOMORROW MORNING

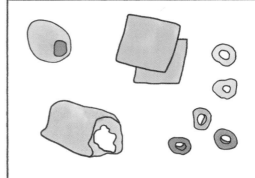

CREATE ELABORATE AND SOPHISTICATED SNACK PLATTERS

LIKE <u>REALLY</u> CLEAN

YOUR SHOWER

MAKE A PLAYLIST FOR
YOUR PLANTS TO PUT ON
WHEN YOU LEAVE THE APT.
WHICH IS NOT OFTEN

SHOP FOR NOSTALGIC ITEMS ONLINE
BECAUSE FOR SOME REASON BEING
SURROUNDED BY SMALL, CUTE, FLUFFY
OR PINK THINGS IS VERY COMFORTING

HI I MISS U ♡

TEXT EVERYONE YOU HAVEN'T TALKED
TO IN AWHILE. LIFE HAS BEEN WEIRD
BUT YOU REALLY DO CARE AND ALSO
MAYBE WANT TO MAKE SURE THEY
HAVEN'T FORGOTTEN ABOUT YOU

IT'S ALMOST LIKE I'D RATHER MAKE UP PAINFUL STORIES IN MY HEAD THAN HANG OUT IN THE UNKNOWN

THERE'S ALWAYS
SOMEONE TO TAKE
A WALK WITH

MY DINNER WOULD BE
PROMPTLY SERVED
EVERY NIGHT

I WOULD LEARN TO
LISTEN AND NOT
TALK SO MUCH

I'M SAVING LOTS OF MONEY ON MY WARDROBE

I CAN PEE OUTSIDE AND IT'S NOT WEIRD

PINEAPPLE IN SMALL AMOUNTS IS SAFE FOR DOGS

← TAP WATER

I'VE GOT NO PRESSURE TO DO LIKE ANYTHING EVER

I COULD SCREAM WHENEVER I WANT TO

HOW TO NOT CHECK YOUR PHONE EVERY 90 SECONDS

HIRE A PRIVATE DOG TRAINER TO TEACH YOUR DOG TO BURY YOUR PHONE IN THE BACKYARD WITH A SIMPLE COMMAND

CAST YOUR HANDS IN PLASTER

DEVELOP AN INVISIBILITY CLOAK PHONE CASE

(THIS WILL PROBABLY ALSO MAKE YOU RICH, WHICH IS COOL)

PACK UP ALL OF YOUR
BELONGINGS, LEAVE YOUR
OLD LIFE BEHIND, AND
MOVE TO THE WOODS WHERE
THERE IS NO CELL SIGNAL
OR WIFI

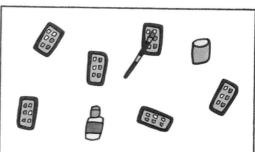

CRAFT MULTIPLE DECOY
PHONES AND PLACE THEM
AROUND YOUR APARTMENT
TO CONFUSE AND FRUSTRATE
YOURSELF ENOUGH TO GIVE
UP THE SEARCH

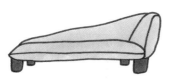

DEDICATE THE NEXT 5+
YEARS IN THERAPY TO
FIGURING OUT WHY YOU
CRAVE SO MUCH EXTERNAL
VALIDATION AND DESIRE A
CONSTANT RUSH OF DOPAMINE

THROW IT OUT THE
WINDOW

WHEN I GET STUCK
IN SHAME

MY BODY FEELS
FROZEN

AND ON FIRE AT
THE SAME TIME

SO HOW CAN I USE THIS FEELING
TO GUIDE ME TOWARD A DEEPER
UNDERSTANDING OF MYSELF?

TO-DO LIST

- MAKE A RELAXING/CALMING PLAYLIST

- WATER PLANTS

- DON'T FORGET THAT THE OK THINGS, THE THINGS THAT I'M AFRAID OF, AND THE BEST THINGS TOO ARE NOT CERTAIN OR GUARANTEED OR FOREVER

Tips & Tricks
to
Avoid the Void

DEVELOP DETAILED ORIGIN STORIES FOR YOUR PLANTS

SEND YOUR MOM A PHOTO OF YOUR NEW GRAY HAIR

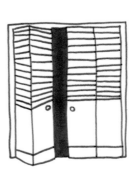

PUT EVERYTHING YOU DON'T LIKE LOOKING AT IN THE CLOSET

MAKE A SMOOTHIE

TAKE 12 VIDEOS OF YOUR DOG JUST LIKE LYING IN BED

PERUSE THE SOCIAL MEDIA ACCOUNTS OF EVERYONE WHO MADE FUN OF YOU IN MIDDLE SCHOOL

GIVE YOURSELF BANGS- YOU WON'T REGRET IT!

Chapter 3
How to Ignore Your Inner Critic

Have you ever listened to what you say to yourself? What does your internal voice sound like? Is it gentle and sweet? Is it encouraging? Providing wholesome pep talks after a difficult day at work or a disagreement with a friend? Do you tell yourself it's going to be okay, you got this, drink some tea, take a bath? Or does it rip apart your every mistake and constantly ridicule you until you're crying and immobile on the floor?

Yeah, that sounds more like it.

To be fair, a really long time ago the primitive human brain learned to do whatever was necessary to be accepted by the tribe and avoid social rejection—otherwise, a saber-toothed tiger would probably eat you. Those were real right?

Life is a little different now, which is great; but we still get scared of rejection, sometimes as if our survival depends on it. Why do we think that being critical of ourselves will protect us from the criticism of others? Does that actually work for you? Because I know it just makes me want to crawl under the covers for an undetermined amount of time.

Self-criticism can feel safe, because then no one else can beat you to it, and this can provide the temporary illusion of control. When I'm stuck in a cycle of negative thinking, I try to keep in mind that I'm doing this to try to protect myself from external pain and failure. But that is impossible, sorry. Being critical of yourself isn't the same as being realistic. It's exhausting when you always assume the worst.

Developing self-compassion isn't about becoming lazy or avoiding accountability. It's about being kind to yourself while you process mistakes and pain and growth and failure. Also, just FYI, being nice to yourself makes it a lot easier to be kind to everyone else you encounter. It rules, because you no longer feel the need to project your internalized judgments and resentment onto those around you. I think that sounds so nice, don't you?

TO-DO LIST

- CLEAN OUT FRIDGE

- RUN THROUGH EVERY POSSIBLE SCENARIO IN MY LIFE WHERE SOMETHING COULD GO WRONG SO I WILL BE PREPARED WHEN IT EVENTUALLY DOES

- CALL MOM

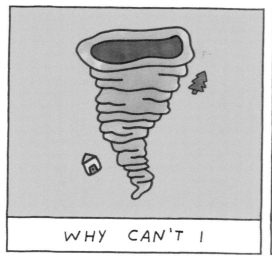

WHY CAN'T I

HAVE THE SAME CONFIDENCE

IN MYSELF THAT

I HAVE IN YOU?

DEAR DIARY,

I'VE NOTICED THAT SOMETIMES I WON'T GO AFTER WHAT I WANT BECAUSE I'M SO SCARED OF WHAT I'LL THINK OF MYSELF IF I DON'T GET IT.

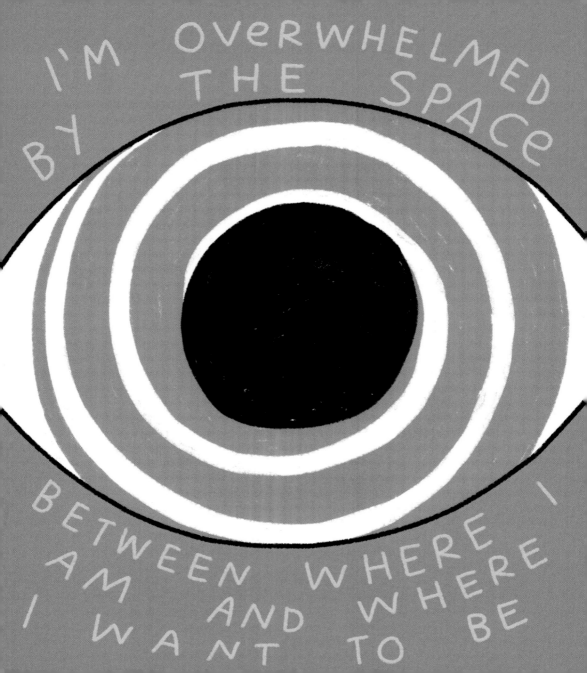

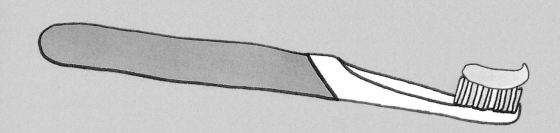

DEAR DIARY,
HEY SO DO YOU
EVER STOP TO THINK
ABOUT ALL THE STUFF
YOU'VE DONE? NOT
IN A "STUCK IN
THE PAST" WAY, BUT
ANYTIME I ACCOMPLISH
A GOAL IT'S LIKE I
IMMEDIATELY MOVE
ON TO THE NEXT
ONE, AND I WANT

TO MAKE MORE
TIME TO TAKE
INVENTORY OF ALL
OF MY EXPERIENCES,
THE CHALLENGING
AND COOL AND
SCARY AND HELPFUL
AND EXCITING AND
EVEN THE REALLY
HARD ONES.

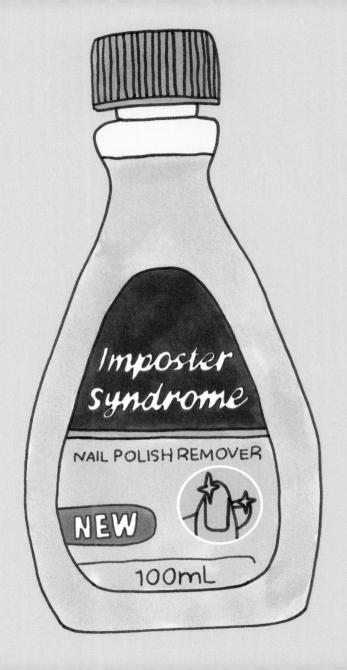

TO-DO LIST

- GYNO VISIT

- PAY RENT

- CONTINUE TO DEVELOP SELF-
COMPASSION BECAUSE IT
HELPS ME TO PRACTICE
COMPASSION FOR EVERYONE
ELSE

DEAR DIARY,
    YOU KNOW
WHAT? WHEN I'M
FEELING AFRAID
OR INSECURE IT'S
SO HARD TO
SEE EVERYTHING
GOOD THAT IS
AROUND ME. HOW
DO I STOP DOING
THAT?

Just Feel Better

**WHEN
YOU'RE**

SAD

HEY COME HERE YEAH YOU SO I HAVE TO TELL YOU SOME-THING OK SO IT'S OK TO LIKE ACTUALLY REALLY LIKE YOUR-SELF OK NO THE TRUTH IS IT'S COOL TO REALLY LIKE YOUR-SELF LIKE SOOOO COOL

DEAR DIARY,
I'VE DECIDED TO
TRY DOING THIS
COOL NEW THING
WHERE I DON'T
JUDGE MYSELF OR
CALL MYSELF
NAMES OR GET
STUCK IN SHAME
WHEN I MAKE
A MISTAKE. MY EGO
WANTS ME TO BELIEVE

THAT IT'S POSSIBLE TO
BE RIGHT ALL OF THE
TIME AND THAT I CAN
AVOID MESSING UP

BUT I DON'T THINK
THAT'S A REALITY FOR
LITERALLY ANYONE

AND I'M TIRED OF
PRETENDING.

THE STORIES YOU KEEP
TELLING YOURSELF

YOU CAN LET THEM GO

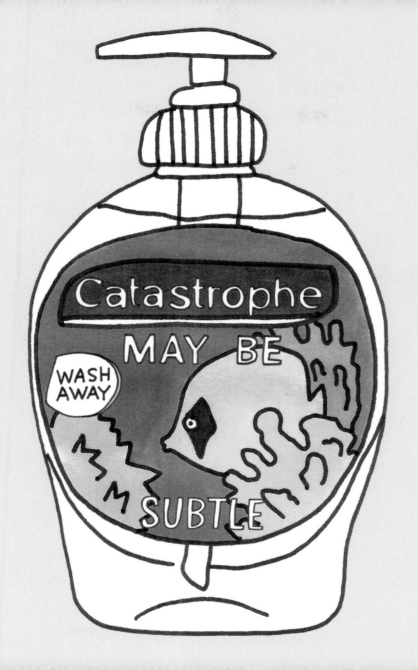

GROCERY LIST

- ALMOND MILK

- KALE

- ACCEPTANCE OF MYSELF REGARDLESS OF MY ACCOMPLISHMENTS

- POP-TARTS

EVEN WHEN I FAIL

AND EXPERIENCE DISAPPOINTMENT OR

REGRET I AM

ALWAYS TRYING MY BEST

IT'S WHAT EVERYBODY KNOWS EXCEPT FOR YOU

HEY! WAIT A MINUTE

WHAT IF LIKE

THERE'S ACTUALLY NOTHING

WRONG WITH ME?

GROCERY LIST

- COOKIES

- ICE CREAM

- THE REALIZATION THAT MY
DEEP FEARS OF SHAME
AND REJECTION ARE MOSTLY
BASED ON A FEW PAINFUL
MOMENTS FROM CHILDHOOD

- CHEESE

- BREAD

113

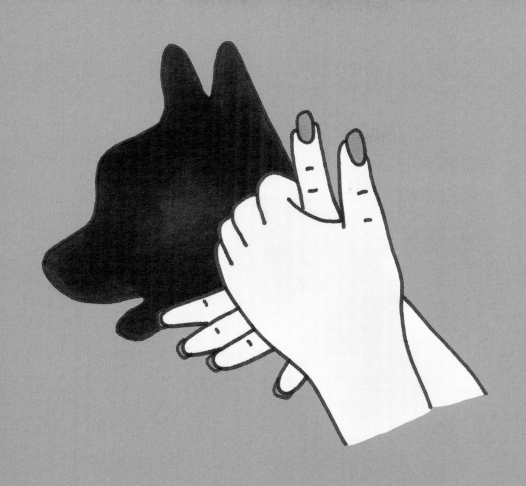

WHY CAN'T YOU JUST STOP THINKING ABOUT IT?

SOME DAYS IT FEELS
BETTER TO PROCRASTINATE

BECAUSE I'M SCARED
THAT IF I ACTUALLY TRY

WHATEVER I COME UP
WITH WILL DISAPPOINT ME

BUT WHAT IF IT
DOESN'T?

DEAR DIARY,
   IS IT NORMAL
TO BE PROUD BUT
ALSO ASHAMED OF
SOMETHING AT THE
SAME TIME? IDK
MAYBE I'M AFRAID
OF BEING JUDGED
FOR EXPRESSING
JOY. WHAT'S THE
DEAL WITH THAT?

TO-DO LIST

- ORDER INK FOR PRINTER

- STOP BY JANIE'S OPENING

- GIVE ALL OF MY ATTENTION
AND FOCUS TO WHAT'S
GOING WRONG IN MY LIFE
AND BARELY REGISTER ALL
THE GOOD STUFF

Chapter 4
How to Feel Connected

You can't know what's really going on in anyone's life. If you try to assume, you will end up comparing your complex self to a flattened, imagined, and assumed version of someone else. I'd like to stop having relationships with fantasized versions of people—it makes me feel pressure to pretend who I am, too. Pretending that everything is okay when it's really not makes me feel so far from other people, when all I want is to feel closer. You're not better or worse than anyone else. We're all just doing the best we can.

You're special and totally deserving of love. Also, your fears and anxieties and desires are universal, they aren't unique. If you can show up in your relationships with the people in your life without trying to bypass the hard stuff, you begin to see that we're not really separate at all.

What do you think is holding you back from being truly seen? What are you trying to hide? Like, have you ever done the thing where you pretended you wanted to do something because you didn't want to disappoint the person you were hanging out with, but then you were just secretly mad the whole time and began to resent them while they had no idea what was going on because they couldn't read your mind? Or what about using humor to deflect anytime a conversation starts to get real? I've *definitely never* done those things, but I think that's how you make sure you don't feel connected to anyone, ever. We need to show up honestly with other people, but we also have to be able to do that with ourselves.

I'm still figuring out the difference between being selfish and honoring my needs. I want to be able to connect with myself and also show up for my community. I'm still figuring out how to build boundaries with people instead of walls. It helps when I remind myself that our relationships with other people, ourselves, ideas, and the whole world don't have to only move in one direction.

TAKE A BREAK

FROM YOURSELF

AND HELP

SOMEONE ELSE

NET WT. 18 OZ. (1 LB. 2 OZ.)

MY TOP 5 CURRENT FEARS ABOUT DATING, MY DOG, & TEAM SPORTS

GETTING INTO A RIDESHARE WITH SOMEONE WHO GHOSTED ME

FORGETTING TO PUT ON PANTS WHEN I TAKE MY DOG FOR A WALK IN THE MORNING

BEING HIT WITH A BASKETBALL IN THE FACE

A FRISBEE FLYING INTO THE BACK OF MY NECK

MAKING EYE CONTACT WITH MY CRUSH AS THEY WALK BY WHILE I'M PICKING UP DOG POOP

(I AM SCARED OF THESE THINGS BECAUSE SOME HAVE ALREADY HAPPENED ONCE BUT YOU HAVE TO GUESS WHICH ONES)

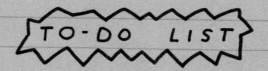

TO-DO LIST

- TAKE TONY ON A LONG WALK

- LUNCH WITH JORDAN AT MᶜCARREN

- ACUPUNCTURE

- REMIND MYSELF THAT IT'S POSSIBLE TO CARE ABOUT YOU AND ALSO TAKE CARE OF MYSELF

I MISS THE VERSION OF YOU
THAT I MADE UP IN MY HEAD
WHEN WE FIRST MET

DEAR DIARY,

WAIT, SO HOW ARE YOU SUPPOSED TO KNOW WHAT YOU WANT OR WHAT IS GOING TO MAKE YOU HAPPY? PLEASE SEND HELP.

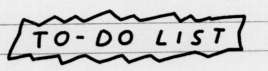

TO-DO LIST

- D.I.Y. PEDICURE

- MAKE SURE THAT EVERYONE KNOWS THAT I AM IN ON THE JOKE AND GENERALLY VERY SELF-AWARE

- BAKE 4 DOZEN PEANUT BUTTER COOKIES

HOW TO REALLY GET TO KNOW YOURSELF

FILL UP A PAGE IN YOUR JOURNAL BEFORE YOU CHECK YOUR PHONE IN THE MORNING

FRIENDS

BEST

FOREVER

ASK SOME OF YOUR FRIENDS WHAT THEIR FAVORITE THING ABOUT YOU IS

MEDITATE

SAY YOUR NAME OUT LOUD
REPEATEDLY UNTIL IT NO
LONGER HAS MEANING AND
IS JUST WEIRD SOUNDS

DO SOME YOGA EVEN IF
YOU'RE REALLY BAD AT IT

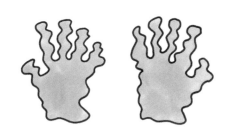

STARE AT YOUR HANDS UNTIL
THE BOUNDARIES BETWEEN YOUR
BODY AND THE ROOM BEGIN TO
BLUR AND NOW YOU CAN SEE HOW
YOU ARE PART OF EVERYTHING
AND EVERYTHING IS PART OF YOU

BUY YOUR FAVORITE FLAVOR OF
ICE CREAM FROM CHILDHOOD
AND EAT 3/4 OF THE TUB IN
ONE NIGHT

SOMETIMES I FEEL LIKE
I'M NOT REAL

GROCERY LIST

- TOMATOES

- BREAD

- AWARENESS AND ACKNOWLEDGMENT OF WHEN I'M HIDING PARTS OF MYSELF FROM OTHERS

- RAINBOW SPRINKLES

ARE YOU AGGRESSIVE, ASSERTIVE, OR AVOIDANT?

A QUICK QUIZ TO HELP YOU FIND OUT HOW YOU RESPOND TO STRESS AND IF THERE IS ANYTHING WRONG WITH YOU

1. A CO-WORKER ASKS YOU A QUESTION THAT YOU DON'T KNOW THE ANSWER TO SO YOU:

A. REPLY "WHY WOULD YOU EVEN ASK ME THAT? WHO CARES?!"

B. SAY "I DON'T KNOW!" WITH A WARM SMILE

C. PRETEND YOU DIDN'T HEAR THEM AND SLOWLY WALK AWAY

2. A FRIEND OFFERS YOU UNSOLICITED ADVICE ON A TOPIC THAT YOU ARE SENSITIVE ABOUT AND THEN YOU:

A. OFFER THEM UNSOLICITED ADVICE ABOUT A TOPIC THAT THEY ARE SENSITIVE ABOUT

B. THANK THEM FOR SHARING THEIR OPINION AND LET THEM KNOW YOU WILL ASK FOR THEIR ADVICE IF YOU WANT IT OR MAYBE JUST SMILE AND NOD

C. AGREE WITH THEM AND ADJUST YOUR LIFE TO THEIR ADVICE SO THAT YOU NEVER HAVE TO THINK ABOUT WHAT YOU REALLY WANT OR NEED

3. YOUR SIGNIFICANT OTHER DOESN'T TEXT YOU BACK FOR A FEW HOURS AND THEN THIS HAPPENS:

A. YOU'RE SINGLE NOW

B. YOU LET THEM KNOW YOU WOULD APPRECIATE A RESPONSE EVEN IF IT'S "HEY I'M BUSY BUT I'LL GET BACK TO YOU LATER" BECAUSE CLEAR COMMUNICATION IS AWESOME

C. YOU SECRETLY HOLD IT AGAINST THEM FOR THE REMAINDER OF YOUR RELATIONSHIP

4. YOU RECEIVE AN EMAIL THAT SAYS "WE NEED TO TALK" FROM A BOSS / LOVER / FRIEND / FAMILY MEMBER SO

A. YOU REPLY IMMEDIATELY ACCUSING THEM OF BEING INCONSIDERATE AND THAT THERE'S A LOT OF STUFF YOU ALSO HAVE TO TALK ABOUT

B. YOU LET THEM KNOW YOUR AVAILABILITY AND DON'T OBSESS OVER WHAT IT MIGHT BE ABOUT BEFORE YOU GET A CHANCE TO TALK

C. YOU THROW YOUR LAPTOP OUT YOUR WINDOW AND LAY IN BED FOR AN UNDISCLOSED AMOUNT OF TIME HOPEFULLY LONG ENOUGH FOR THIS PERSON TO FORGET ABOUT YOU

TURN THE PAGE UPSIDE DOWN TO SEE YOUR RESULTS!

IF YOU ANSWERED MOSTLY A's YOU ARE AGGRESSIVE AND MAYBE EVERYONE IS NOT OUT TO GET YOU? B's YOU ARE ASSERTIVE AND KIND OF WINNING AT LIFE RIGHT NOW C's YOU ARE AVOIDANT AND COULD TRY BEING LESS AFRAID OF EVERYONE AND EVERYTHING AROUND YOU

OH, YES, HI,
HELLO, COULD
YOU TELL ME
WHAT KEEPS
GETTING IN
THE WAY OF
LOVE?

IF I WAIT TOO LONG TO SAY HOW I REALLY FEEL

DEAR DIARY,
WOULDN'T IT BE
SO COOL TO
ALWAYS BE ABLE
TO SHARE YOUR
FEELINGS AND THOUGHTS
WITH OTHER PEOPLE
AND NOT BE
ABSOLUTELY TERRIFIED
THAT THEY WON'T
AGREE OR UNDERSTAND?

Love Sonnet XV

GRACE MICELI, 1988–

I LIKE TO
WATCH YOUR
STORIES

THE INTERNET
ON MY
LAPTOP
MORE

43 SECONDS
AFTER YOU
POST THEM
AND

I THINK THAT
I COULD HEAR

I CAN'T DECIDE
IF I PREFER

THE SOUND
OF YOUR
TEXT MESSAGE

THE INTERNET
ON MY
PHONE
OR

EVEN FROM
A MILE
AWAY

MY TOP 5 CURRENT FEARS ABOUT RUNNING ERRANDS, WEARING CLOTHES, AND CONTEMPLATING MY FUTURE

I AM COOL

I AM COOL

MAKING A DEPOSIT AT THE BANK WITH MY SKIRT TUCKED INTO MY UNDERWEAR

WAITING AT A BUS STOP NEXT TO SOMEONE WEARING THE SAME T-SHIRT AS ME

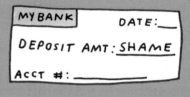

MY BANK   DATE:___
DEPOSIT AMT: SHAME
ACCT #: _____

NEVER BEING ABLE TO FIGURE OUT WHAT MAKES ME TRULY HAPPY

4:20 START

NEXT CUSTOMER

LOSING MY MOM AT THE GROCERY STORE WITH NO CELL SERVICE AT AGE 31

BEING STUCK IN A LONG LINE BEHIND AN OLD ROOMMATE WHO I NEVER REALLY GOT ALONG WITH

HOW TO HAVE FEELINGS (AFTER YOU PRETENDED THAT YOU DIDN'T FOR ALMOST 20 YEARS)

I DON'T REMEMBER EXACTLY WHEN OR WHY I STARTED TO BELIEVE THAT IT WASN'T OK TO HAVE FEELINGS OR EXPRESS EMOTIONS

((◖ ◗ ○ ○ ◖))

MAYBE IT HAPPENED SLOWLY OVER TIME OR MAYBE I WOKE UP ONE DAY UNDERSTANDING THAT THIS WAS HOW IT HAD TO BE

THERE WAS A TERRIFYING SWIRL OF THINGS INSIDE OF ME

ENDOMETRIOSIS
CRUSHES
1,000 UNREQUITED
RAGE
SHAME
DIET DR. PEPPER FOR BREAKFAST
FEAR
BRACES
LONELINESS

145

WELCOME TO
FEELINGS 101

THIS WOULD HAVE
BEEN A HELPFUL
CLASS IN MIDDLE
SCHOOL

BUT IT WASN'T, AND I
BEGAN TO PUT THEM
ALL AWAY

IDK
I THOUGHT THAT
IT WOULD KEEP
ME SAFE

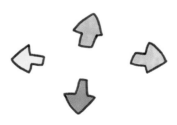

SOMETIMES I WOULD PUSH
MY FEELINGS DOWN AND
SOMETIMES TO THE SIDE
OR BEHIND ME TOO

CERTAIN EMOTIONS RESISTED MORE THAN OTHERS, BUT I'M A QUICK LEARNER

I GUESS IN THE MOMENT IT FELT BETTER

OTHER PEOPLE'S FEELINGS BECAME EMBARASSING TOO.

I NEVER KNEW WHAT TO DO OR SAY WHEN CONFRONTED WITH THEM

I CONVINCED MYSELF THAT I WAS LUCKY TO NOT BE ONE OF THOSE "EMOTIONAL PEOPLE." I TOOK PRIDE IN MY EMPTINESS. I THOUGHT IT MADE ME STRONGER BUT MY HEART GOT SO SMALL

AS THE YEARS
WENT BY
IT BECAME
HARDER
TO KEEP MY
FEELINGS
QUIET

I HAD TO FIND MORE
WAYS TO KEEP THEM
HIDDEN, THEY WERE
GETTING LOUDER

THERE WASN'T
ANYWHERE FOR
MY EMOTIONS
TO GO

WHEN YOU PUSH
AWAY THE SCARY
STUFF, YOU PUSH
AWAY THE NICE
STUFF TOO, AND
ALL OF IT
BEGINS TO DULL

HOW DO YOU CONNECT
WITH ANYONE WHEN
YOU DON'T KNOW
HOW TO BE
YOURSELF?

I WASN'T SURE IF
I COULD KEEP
GOING

ALMOST
ME

BUT I DECIDED THAT
I WANTED TO KEEP
TRYING AND THEN
SOMEONE (MY NEW
THERAPIST) TOLD ME
A SECRET THAT I
GUESS A LOT OF
PEOPLE ALREADY KNEW

IF YOU LET YOURSELF
FEEL WHATEVER
COMES UP AND STAY
PRESENT IT DOESN'T
USUALLY LAST THAT
LONG

I BECAME KIND OF
OBSESSED WITH CRYING.
I WOULD TELL EVERYONE
WHAT I WAS FEELING
ALL OF THE TIME

GRACE
HAD A
FEELING

WHAT A RELIEF TO
KNOW THAT I COULD
HAVE A BIG AND FULL
AND MESSY LIFE TOO

I'M STILL FIGURING
IT OUT,
HOW TO FEEL
THINGS WITHOUT
LETTING THEM
CONSUME ME

AND SOMETIMES
I STILL RUN
AWAY, BUT
USUALLY I'M
ABLE TO STAY
AND I THINK
THAT IS JUST
SO COOL

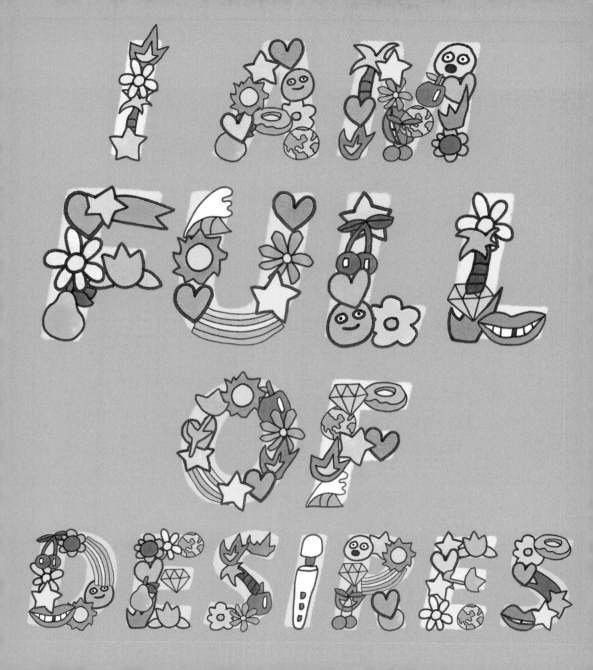

WHEN EVERYTHING SEEMS OK EVEN JUST FOR A LITTLE BIT

LISTENING TO THE OCEAN WHEN THE SKY IS PINK

TEXTING SOMEONE "I LOVE YOU" JUST BECAUSE

ORDERING STUFF ONLINE BECAUSE THEN THERE IS SOMETHING TO LOOK FORWARD TO

READING A BOOK WHILE YOU FALL ASLEEP AND THEN AGAIN DURING BREAKFAST

MAKING EYE CONTACT WITH A DOG FROM ACROSS THE ROOM

AWE SOME BOOK

IT'S SO COOL
THAT I FEEL
SAFE WHEN
I'M WITH YOU

I'M AFRAID TO

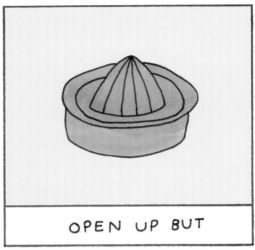

OPEN UP BUT

IT'S ALWAYS WORTH IT

WHEN I SHARE HOW I FEEL

WHAT I WAS ACTUALLY TRYING TO SAY

SOMETIMES IT'S NICE TO REMEMBER

THAT YOU
ARE SMALL

DEAR DIARY,
  I WANT TO
LEARN TO BE OK
WITH DISAPPOINTING
PEOPLE. WHY IS
IT SO HARD TO
SIT WITH
NEGATIVE
  EMOTIONS? LMK

What Am I Really Afraid of?

ONE-SIDED CONVERSATIONS I'VE HAD WITH MY DOG

IT'S A GOOD IDEA TO NOT LEAVE BED TODAY, LMK IF YOU DISAGREE

SHOULD I HAVE PIE OR ICE CREAM FOR DINNER?

IT'S COOL THAT YOU THINK YOU'RE IN CHARGE EVEN THOUGH YOU'RE SMALLER THAN MY THIGH

I WONDER IF LIFE WILL EVER FEEL NORMAL AGAIN

DO YOU THINK IT'S TOO HOT OUT TO WEAR PANTS?

I KNOW SOMETIMES I TALK A LOT (ABOUT MYSELF)

I'M SORRY ABOUT THAT, I DON'T WANT THE ATTENTION OR TO TAKE UP SO MUCH SPACE

I'M TRYING TO SHARE MYSELF WITH YOU BECAUSE I HOPE THAT BY OPENING UP

YOU WILL FEEL COMFORTABLE ENOUGH TO OPEN UP TO ME TOO

GROCERY LIST

- KEWPIE

- DEEPER UNDERSTANDING OF HOW WE CAN SHARE AN EXPERIENCE (LIKE BE IN THE SAME PLACE AT THE SAME TIME) YET PERCEIVE WHAT HAPPENS IN VERY DIFFERENT WAYS

- SPAM

DEAR DIARY,
 HEY WHAT'S UP, IT'S
ME AGAIN. I DON'T
WANT TO RUN AWAY
EVERY TIME THE FANTASY
VERSION OF SOMEONE
FALLS APART AND I
REALIZE THEY ARE
MESSY, CONFUSED,
SCARED, AND
COMPLICATED JUST LIKE
ME.

165

A girl @ Night on the internet

(AN EXTREMELY SIMPLIFIED VERSION OF SOMETHING I THINK ABOUT EVERY SINGLE DAY)

</3

I COULDN'T BELIEVE THAT I HAD FOUND THIS PORTAL TO NEW PLACES AND PEOPLE AND IDEAS

THERE WAS CONNECTION AND KNOWLEDGE AND EXCITEMENT AND SO MUCH TO SEE

I ♥ THE ENDLESS SCROLL

FOR THE FIRST TIME I FELT LIKE I WAS ME AND THAT I WAS SEEN AND WE BUILT SO MANY THINGS!

BUT THEN WITHOUT REALIZING IT
I BECAME WHO I WAS
ONLINE AND NOT SO MUCH
A PERSON IN THE WORLD

ME
↓
_____

MY PHYSICALITY WAS AN
AFTERTHOUGHT

I HAVE TO FIND MY
WAY BACK

SOME DAYS I
STILL DREAM
OF ESCAPING

I REALLY HOPE THERE IS A
WAY TO FEEL WHOLE WITHOUT
CHASING THE DOPAMINE RUSH
I GET WHEN A STRANGER
ON THE INTERNET SAYS
THAT I AM GOOD BY
CLICKING ON A TINY HEART
BUT I DON'T KNOW IT YET
BECAUSE I CHECKED MY
INSTAGRAM TWICE WHILE
WRITING THIS SENTENCE
BUT IF YOU DO COULD YOU
SEND ME AN EMAIL?

Everyone Feels So Far Away

Chapter 5
How to Keep Going

Sometimes I like to use the helpful tools I've learned against myself. Have you ever tried to be an overachiever when it comes to growth and healing? It's the worst. You don't have to "unlock your hidden potential" or "turn your life around." There's not a perfect version of yourself that you need to transform into. I think growth is more about figuring out how to reframe how you look at the world and talk to yourself, so you can figure out how to exist in this current reality. It's about getting through today without feeling like you can't handle tomorrow. It's about gaining insight and collecting tools for your symbolic-but-like-totally-real tool kit. And just maybe, it's about trying to figure out a way to enjoy life, too.

For me, being a better version of myself means I won't check my phone while I'm in the middle of a conversation with someone who is standing in front of me, or I will make my bed in the morning, or correct people when they mispronounce my name. I will try to focus on the small changes I can make, because all together they add up. Goals and dreams are awesome because they provide a path to follow and a reason to wake up in the morning, but I know that I also want to look back at my life and be like, "Yeah, cool, I was actually paying attention for most of that."

Can you loosen your grip a little? Who and what can you surround yourself with that inspires you to open up, for your heart to grow even bigger so you can be a kinder version of yourself? There are so many ways to live a life, but I'm guessing that you don't want to feel so scared anymore. It is possible to listen and learn from others while not fixating on trying to make everyone around you happy.

Some periods of your life might require more maintenance and effort, but once you figure out what is helpful to you (that tool kit I just mentioned) there should be stretches of time where it gets a little easier. And yeah, it's kind of annoying that your problems won't magically be solved just because you know better and are aware of what's really going on now. Every day is an opportunity to practice what you've learned, and I'm going to choose to be hopeful and excited by that, or at least I'm going to try. Want to join me?

NOW WHAT DO I DO WITH ALL OF THIS AWARENESS

IT'S OK TO NOT
THINK ABOUT ALL
OF THE STUFF ALL
OF THE TIME

SELF-ACTUALIZATION

ESTEEM

LOVE

SAFETY

PHYSIOLOGICAL

ACTUALLY NOT TAKING THINGS PERSONALLY BECAUSE WE ALL HAVE STUFF GOING ON AND SOMETIMES WE ACCIDENTALLY TAKE IT OUT ON EACH OTHER

BEING NICE TO YOURSELF ON DAYS WHEN YOU ACCOMPLISH NOTHING

ADOPTING A SMALL DOG

FALLING ASLEEP WITHOUT CHECKING YOUR CLOSETS, UNDER YOUR BED, BEHIND YOUR SHOWER CURTAIN OR INSIDE YOUR CABINETS

DRINKING WATER THAT'S NOT SELTZER

HIERARCHY OF NEEDS

YOU WILL MESS IT UP

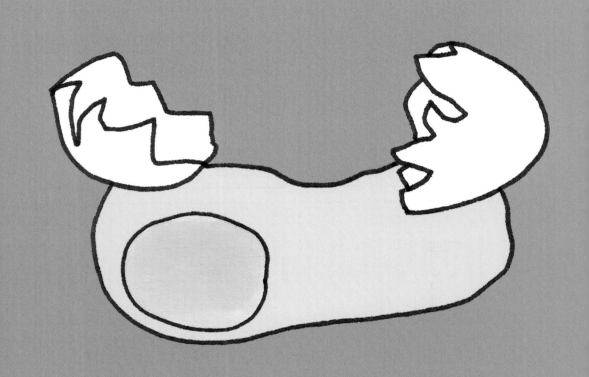

BUT NOT EVERY TIME

SOME THINGS HAVE

NOT WORKED OUT

IN THE WAY THAT

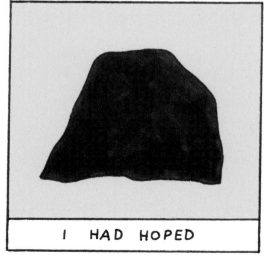

I HAD HOPED

GROCERY LIST

- SHISHITO PEPPERS

- GARLIC

- PURPLE CABBAGE

- AN APOLOGY TO MYSELF
FOR DOING ALL THE THINGS
THAT I DIDN'T WANT TO DO

MY ANGER SHOWS ME WHEN THERE IS SOMETHING IN THE WAY OF MY NEEDS BEING MET

How to Try and Make Sense of Thoughts vs. Feelings

I'M CALM
IS A FEELING.

EVERYONE IS LOOKING
AT ME IS A THOUGHT.

I'M EMBARRASSED
IS A FEELING.

MY FRIEND DIDN'T TEXT ME BACK IN 24 HRS SO THEY MUST HATE ME <u>IS A THOUGHT</u>.

I'M DISAPPOINTED <u>IS A FEELING</u>.

I NEED TO BE IN CONTROL <u>IS A THOUGHT</u>.

I'M ENRAGED <u>IS A FEELING</u>.

NO ONE CARES ABOUT
ME IS A THOUGHT.

I'LL NEVER FIGURE OUT WHAT
I WANT IS A THOUGHT.

I HAVE SO MUCH TO LEARN
ABOUT MYSELF IS A THOUGHT.

I'M HOPEFUL
IS A FEELING.

GROCERY LIST

- CURIOSITY ABOUT ALL OF THE THINGS THAT I AUTOMATICALLY ASSUME TO BE TRUE

- BANANAS

- PEANUT BUTTER

I'M SORRY I WILL TRY TO BE
LESS RIGID MOVING FORWARD

DEAR DIARY,
TODAY I WAS GOING TO VACUUM MY KITCHEN AND WORK OUT AND MEDITATE AND EAT VEGETABLES AND SEND ALL THESE WORK EMAILS AND TAKE MY DOG ON A REALLY LONG WALK, BUT INSTEAD

I WATCHED FOUR
MOVIES AND ATE A
PINT OF ICE
CREAM FOR LUNCH.
EVEN THOUGH I
KNOW ALL THE THINGS
TO DO THAT WILL
HELP ME FEEL
BETTER SOME DAYS
I JUST DON'T DO THEM.

What Really Matters?

ONE-PLY

4 Rolls

GROCERY LIST

- HOT DOGS

- MUSTARD

- AT LEAST 4 KINDS OF POTATO CHIPS

- THE ABILITY TO SHIFT MY PERSPECTIVE AND ZOOM OUT TO CHANGE MY VIEW WHEN I'M FEELING OVERWHELMED

TO-DO LIST

- DROP PACKAGES AT POST OFFICE

- VOCALIZE MY NEEDS AND BOUNDARIES EVEN THOUGH I'M SCARED HOW OTHERS MAY REACT TO THEM

- TAKE OUT TRASH

HOW TO ALLEVIATE PAIN
FROM SMARTPHONE USE

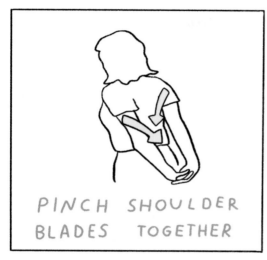

PINCH SHOULDER
BLADES TOGETHER

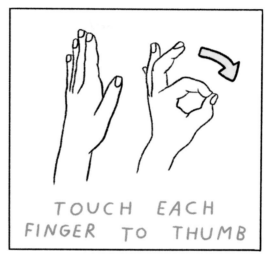

TOUCH EACH
FINGER TO THUMB

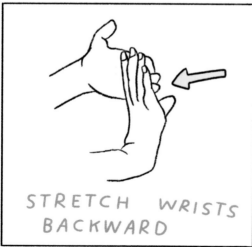

STRETCH WRISTS
BACKWARD

SMASH HAMMER INTO
PHONE AND/OR HAND

HAVING A SCHEDULE HELPS TO KEEP ME MOTIVATED AND NOT FEEL LIKE I'M JUST FLOATING AROUND AND IF I DON'T GET TO EVERYTHING I TAKE IT EASY ON MYSELF
11 12 1 2 3 4 5 6 7 8 9 10

GETTING WHAT < WANTING IT
YOU WANT

BEING KNOWN > A MYSTERY

MESS > ORDER

WONDERING > KNOWING

A FAVOR < THE FAVOR
RETURNED

REMEMBERING ≠ NOT
FORGETTING

TELLING A < BEING TOLD
SECRET A SECRET

TRYING = A TRAP
TO ALWAYS
BE GOOD AT IT

A LITTLE BIT > TOO MUCH

ANXIETY = SOMETHING
TO DO

SOMETIMES YOU END UP

RUNNING VERY FAR
AWAY FROM

WHERE YOU THOUGHT

YOU WANTED TO BE

TO-DO LIST

- PROCRASTINATE SOMETHING THAT WOULD TAKE AROUND 20 MINUTES FOR ANYWHERE FROM 5 HOURS UP TO 6 MONTHS

- SEPARATE RECYCLING

- SEND A "THANK YOU" CARD TO GRANDMA

There Is Always Going to Be Something

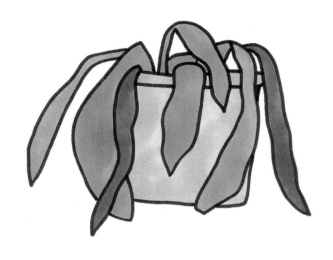

I WANT TO FEEL IT ALL BUT
I'M SCARED THAT ONCE I START
IT WILL BE HARD TO STOP

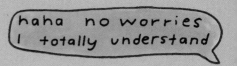

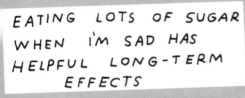

SOME DAYS ARE WONDERFUL

AND SOME DAYS
ARE NOT

ONCE I REALIZED THAT I WILL
NEVER STOP CHANGING OR
GROWING THE WORLD BECAME
A LOT LESS SCARY

What's Next?

Resources

I'm privileged to have the opportunity to learn from numerous teachers, artists, mental health professionals, and authors. This book isn't full of any new ideas, it's a compilation of what others have taught me and how my brain has made sense of the wisdom that I've been lucky enough to encounter. My psychoeducation and spiritual practice will forever be in flux and I can't wait to keep learning.

Below is a list of people, books, and podcasts that continue to inform the artwork I create, how I perceive the world, and the way I try to live my life, check them out if you're feeling curious:

Radical Compassion by Tara Brach

When Things Fall Apart by Pema Chödrön

Josh Korda/Dharmapunx NYC

The Four Agreements by Don Miguel Ruiz

Psychology Today (I found my therapist here)

Feel the Fear...and Do It Anyway by Susan Jeffers

The Artist's Way by Julia Cameron

Facing Love Addiction by Pia Mellody

Bunny Michael

The Body Keeps the Score by Bessel van der Kolk

Nedra Glover Tawwab

All About Love by bell hooks

Lama Rod Owens

Yumi Sakugawa

Terrible, Thanks For Asking

Miranda July

Codependent No More by Melody Beattie

Melissa Broder

Kara Loewentheil

No Feeling Is Final

Where Should We Begin? with Esther Perel

The Mental Illness Happy Hour with Paul Gilmartin

Feel It Out by Jordan Sondler

Acknowledgments

Thank you to my agent, Kate Woodrow, for being such a champion of me and this book. I had no idea what I was doing at first, but your confidence was contagious.

Thank you to my editor, Emma Brodie, for your excitement and ability to truly see me.

Thank you to Augusta for pushing me to do so many things I was afraid of, you were right, it's usually never as scary as it seems in my head.

Thank you to Nick for your love and for making me laugh so much through all of this, and for walking Tony late at night when I didn't want to put on pants.

Jordan and Adam, thank you for being my book fairy godparents, for convincing me that I could do this and for eating pizza with me. I am so inspired by you both.

Mom, Dad, and Gianni, thanks for giving me so much to talk about in therapy. Thank you for thinking it's cool that I wanted to be an artist, you're all so creative in your own ways.

Aleia, I'm so thankful that we found each other and are connected in a sometimes scary but mostly incredible way.

LZ and Dory and everyone from Smith College, thanks for being there for me before I went back to therapy, I have so much love for you.

Brooke, you're always going to feel like a sister to me, I love you.

Fabi, I can't wait to work on something big and beautiful together one day, you are so special.

India, Janie, KJW, Jacob Berry, Keara Price, Erik Sutch, Becky Iasillo, Alex Wallbaum, Tatum Mangus, Cady Chaplin, Jeffery Santos, Lisa Schrader, Ambar Navarro, Emma Byström, Samantha Rothenberg and Katie Pellico – thank you for your support, care and company over the years, you're all so awesome.

Thank you to all of the artists I had the pleasure to work with during the days of Art Baby Gallery, you were my home and community on the internet for so long, I'll never forget that.

About the Author

Photo by Tatum Mangus

Grace Miceli (aka @artbabygirl) is one of the "9 Funniest Cartoonists and Illustrators on Instagram" (*Vulture*). Her artwork has been featured in more than 50 galleries and museums worldwide; she has created work for *The New Yorker*, the *New York Times*, Apple TV, Urban Outfitters, and Nike, and has been covered by *Vogue,* i-D, *Dazed*, CNN, and more. Grace lives in Brooklyn.